Flying

3 5988 00037 0416

by **Dana Meachen Rau**

Reading Consultant: Nanci R. Vargus, Ed. D.

Marshall Cavendish
Benchmark
New York

Picture Words

airplane

bee

bird

butterfly

city

clouds

flower

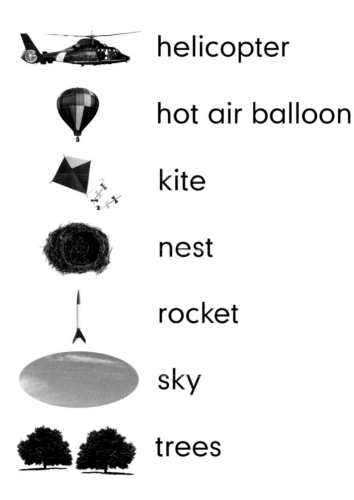

helicopter

hot air balloon

kite

nest

rocket

sky

trees

3

Look up.

Many things can fly in the .

A 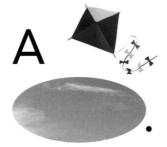 flies in the .

It flies in the wind.

A  flies in the .

It flies over the.

A  flies in the .

It flies over a .

A  flies in the .

It flies over the .

A  flies in the .

It flies to a .

14

A  flies in the .

It flies to a 🌼.

16

A  flies in the .

It flies to a , too.

You can fly in the .

You can fly in an .

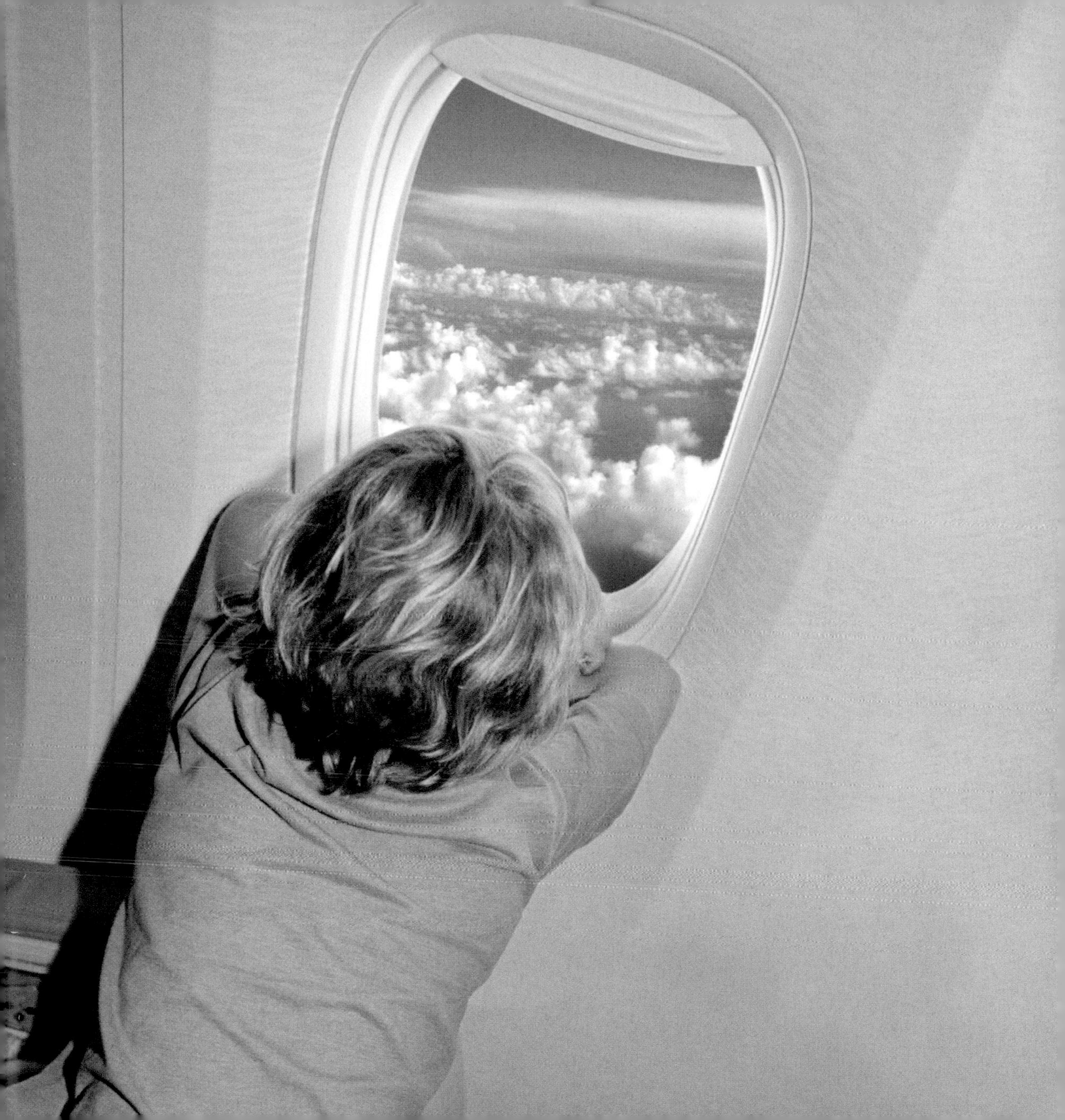

Words to Know

fly   (fleye)
to move in the air

wind moving air

Find Out More

Books

Lin, Grace. *Kite Flying*. New York: Alfred A. Knopf, 2002.

Rogers, Hal. *Rescue Machines at Work: Rescue Helicopters*. Chanhassen, MN: The Child's World, Inc., 2000.

Schuh, Mari C. *Butterflies*. Mankato, MN: Pebble Books, 2003.

Walker, Pamela. *Plane Rides* (Welcome Books). Danbury, CT: Children's Press, 2000.

Videos

Nye, Bill. *Birds*. Disney Educational Productions, 2003.

Web Sites

Benjamin Franklin: Make a Kite
http://www.pbs.org/benfranklin/exp_kite.html

eBALLOON.ORG
http://www.eballoon.org/index.html

Smithsonian National Air and Space Museum
http://www.nasm.si.edu/

About the Author

Dana Meachen Rau is an author, editor, and illustrator. A graduate of Trinity College in Hartford, Connecticut, she has written more than one hundred books for children, including nonfiction, biographies, early readers, and historical fiction. She lives in Burlington, Connecticut, and likes to fly in airplanes when she goes on vacation.

About the Reading Consultant

Nanci R. Vargus, Ed.D, wants all children to enjoy reading. She used to teach first grade. Now she works at the University of Indianapolis. Nanci helps young people become teachers. Her longest airplane trip took twenty-five hours! She flew from Indianapolis to the Philippine Islands.

Marshall Cavendish Benchmark
99 White Plains Road
Tarrytown, NY 10591-9001
www.marshallcavendish.us

All Internet sites were correct at the time of printing.

Library of Congress Cataloging-in-Publication Data

Rau, Dana Meachen, 1971–
       p. cm. — (Benchmark rebus)
Summary: "Easy to read text with rebuses explores various things that fly"—Provided by publisher.
Includes bibliographical references.
ISBN-13: 978-0-7614-2319-5
ISBN-10: 0-7614-2319-2
Flight—Juvenile literature. 2. Rebuses—Juvenile literature. 3. Vocabulary—Juvenile literature. I. Title. II. Series.
TL547.R352006
629.13—dc22
       2005032991

Editor: Christine Florie
Editorial Director: Michelle Bisson
Art Director: Anahid Hamparian
Series Designer: Virginia Pope

Photo research by Connie Gardner

Rebus images, with the exception of the hot air balloon and the helicopter provided courtesy of *Dorling Kindersley*. Toy space rocket and nest © Stephen Oliver/*Dorling Kindersley*.

The photographs in this book are used with permission and through the courtesy of:
Corbis: cover photo Royalty-Free; rebus image p. 3 Royalty-Free; p. 5 Laura Doss; p. 7 Roy Morsch/zefa; p. 9 Bob Krist; p. 11 Reuters; p. 13 Bettmann; p. 19 F. Rauschenbach/zefa; *The Image Works*: p. 15 UNEP/Say Boon Foo; *Peter Arnold*: p. 17 Alan and Sandy Carey; *Getty*: p. 21 Marina Jefferson/The Image Bank.

Printed in Malaysia
1 3 5 6 4 2